Nelson

Handwriting

Pupil Book 3

Nelson

D1335708

Look at these letters and numerals.

Lower case letters for handwriting

a b c d e f g h i j k l m n
o p q r s t u v w x y z

Capital letters

A B C D E F G H I J K L M N O P Q R S T U
V W X Y Z

Numerals

0 1 2 3 4 5 6 7 8 9

Copy the letters and numerals.
Check your writing against the page.

Remember to slope your writing slightly to the right.

The joins are based on the upswing in the swings pattern. First, practise the swings pattern until you can make it evenly, smoothly and quickly.

*uuuuuuu uuuuuuu uuuuuuu
uuuuuuu uuuuuuu uuuuuuu*

Now check that you remember how to make each type of join. Practise these words several times and check that you have made the joins correctly. You need to be able to write these words smoothly, evenly and easily.

The first join
Set 1 to Set 2

am

came dame den had ham

lace made main man name

The second join
Set 1 to Set 3

ul

bulk cake chalk duck dull

mail milk tail talk think

The third join
Set 4 to Set 2

ow

crowd done rent rovers

vote vow warn wave went

The fourth join
Set 4 to Set 3

rb

barber bother flock lark

pool cork stroll whale

The break letters

boxes yellow gold jumbo

press queen razor rubber

Letters may slope forward slightly but they must all have the same slope. The slope should not be more than this:

parallel lines

You will not find it difficult to keep the right slope if you turn your paper at an angle and pull the pen strokes in the right direction.

Hold your pen lightly about 3cm from the point.

Do not alter your grip or the angle of the nib when you are writing.

Practise making these patterns quickly and smoothly. Try to slope them slightly to the right.

eeeee   eeeee   ɹɹɹɹɹ   ɹɹɹɹɹ

wwww   wwww   wwww   wwww

uuuu   uuuu   uuuu   uuuu

uuuw   uuuw   uuuw   uuuw

mmm   mmm   mmm   mmm

Copy this description in your best writing.
Slope your writing slightly to the right, bearing in mind the advice given on page 4.

The Oak Tree

The English oak tree has green leaves which grow on short stalks. The leaves are oval but the edges are wavy. The fruits are acorns which grow in little cups with long stalks. These acorns and cups are green at first but turn brown by autumn.

Copy these poems in your best sloping handwriting.

Tree

Swaying in the wind,
I catch people's attention.
I begin to wave,
They never wave back to me,
I think nobody likes me.

by Dominic Dowell

The Trees

I saw
Two old oak trees
Playing with a ball; One
Threw it in the other's branches,
And laughed.

by Jane Alden

December Leaves

The fallen leaves are cornflakes
That fill the lawn's white dish,
And night and noon
The wind's a spoon
That stirs them with a swish.

The sky's a silver sifter,
A-sifting white and slow
That gently shakes
On crisp brown flakes
The sugar known as snow.

by Kaye Starbird

Does your writing slope correctly?

Many words contain the letters *gh*.
The two are never joined.

g is a break letter.

That night the moonlight was very bright.

Copy this.

ight ight ight ight ight

igh always sounds like the *ie* in *pie*.

Copy these words.

fight light might right tight bright fright flight plight slight

Copy each of these words.
Choose an *ight* word that means the same thing from the box above.

1 close-fitting   2 small

3 shiny   4 flying

Write two words that **end** with *igh*.

5 fear   6 correct

I take it you already know
Of tough and bough and
cough and dough?

When *ou* goes before *gh* it can make several different sounds.

Copy these words.

> bough   dough   tough
> rough   cough   enough
> bought   through
> sought   plough
> although   brought

Write the *ough* words.

1   *ough* sounds like *ow* in *cow* in the word _____ bough

2   *ough* sounds like *aw* in *raw* in the word _____

3   *ough* sounds like *uff* in *cuff* in the word _____

4   *ough* sounds like *off* in *toff* in the word _____

5   *ough* sounds like *ow* in *mow* in the word _____

6   *ough* sounds like *oo* in *too* in the word _____

a tackle

a temple

Sometimes the le ending is joined to the letter that goes before it.
Sometimes the letter that goes before it is a break letter.

Copy these words.

buckle bundle battle kettle knuckle candle
idle needle pickle little settle tackle

Make a chart like this. Write the words above in the correct columns.

–ckle	–ttle	–dle

Choose ngle, ble or ple to finish each of the words below.
Write the completed words in your best writing.

1 a _____   2 edi _____   3 exam _____

4. pur _____   5 mi _____   6 possi _____

7 reasona _____   8 stra _____   9 tem _____

10 sta _____   11 tram _____   12 si _____

valuable candle buckle impossible bangle legible cattle people

Choose a word or words from the box to complete each sentence.
Write the sentences.

1 The farmer had a lot of _____ in his field.

2 Rina knew that her silver _____ was _____.

3 Most _____ try to make their handwriting _____.

4 There was so much traffic that it was _____ to cross the road.

5 The cave was lit by the light of a _____.

6 The _____ on my belt was broken.

In verbs that end with a break letter, take care when you add *ing* or *ed*.

dig digging

The pirate is digging for gold.

Make a chart like this.
Complete the chart in your best handwriting.

rub	rubbing	rubbed
grab		
beg		
jog		
hop		
trap		

With all these verbs you have to double the last letter before you add *ing* or *ed*.

Make up three sentences using some of these verbs.
Write the sentences.

In verbs that end with a consonant + *e*
we drop the *e* before adding *ing* or *ed*.
Make a chart like this.
Complete the chart in your best handwriting.

rake	raking	raked
smile		
slice		
wave		
live		
tame		

Now do the same with this chart.

describe	describing	described
probe		
stage		
tape		
wipe		
graze		
amaze		

Take care!
All these verbs
contain break
letters.

13

A conjunction is used to join two simple sentences to make a compound sentence.

I like pizza <u>but</u> my sister likes hot dogs.

Copy these sentences.
Underline the conjunctions.

1 Would you like chocolate ice cream or would you prefer strawberry?

2 I could not play for the football team because I had hurt my leg.

3 We thought our new teacher was nice although she was rather strict.

4 You have to buy a ticket before you can get on the train.

5 We will go to the beach if the weather is fine.

14

| although | when | or | so that |
| where | before | if |

Choose a conjunction from the box to join each of these pairs of simple sentences. Write the compound sentences and underline the conjunctions.

1 The soldiers are wearing camouflaged uniforms. They will be difficult to see.

2 We could play cricket.
We could play rounders.

3 We were on the way to the park.
We met our friends.

4 I will go to the school play with you.
You will promise not to wear that shirt.

5 I enjoy hot weather. It makes me feel tired.

6 The fox was in the wood. We saw a deer.

7 I put my wellingtons on.
I went out in the snow.

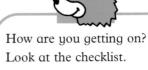

How are you getting on?
Look at the checklist.
Keep practising!

15

they   them   we

A pronoun is used in place of a noun.

Read this story.

Abbie and Scott asked their mother if <u>Abbie and Scott</u> could take a picnic to the park. Their mother agreed, and put some cola in a bag for <u>Abbie and Scott</u>. Abbie and Scott took their skateboards and their picnic and hurried to the park. <u>Abbie and Scott</u> met some of their friends in the park. Their friends said, "Can <u>your friends</u> have a go on your skateboards?" Abbie and Scott agreed, and let their friends share their picnic.

Write the story, using *they*, *them* or *we* instead of the words which are underlined.

16

| him | her | yours | he | mine |
| she | ours | it | you | |

Write these sentences, using one of the pronouns above instead of each of the words or groups of words which are underlined.

1 Jessica said to Lee, "<u>Lee</u> will be late."

2 Ranjit asked the other boys if <u>Ranjit</u> could join the game.

3 Dominic was watching a cartoon but <u>the cartoon</u> bored <u>Dominic</u>.

4 Rina asked <u>Rina's</u> mother if <u>Rina</u> could have a chocolate biscuit.

5 Zoe said, "That pencil is <u>Zoe's</u>."

6 Amy and Matthew said, "That tape is <u>Amy's and Matthew's</u>."

7 Rebecca said to Emma, "Is this doll <u>Emma's</u>?"

The 19th century saw a great revolution in medicine, with many new scientific discoveries being made. Surgeons carried out a wider range of operations than ever before. In 1846 Peter Squire gave ether anaesthetic to a patient while his leg was being amputated. The patient remained unconscious throughout and felt no pain.

Later in the 19th century the work of three medical scientists – Louis Pasteur, Robert Koch and Joseph Lister – led to the discovery that bacteria were the cause of infection in wounds after an operation.

A paragraph is a group of sentences about the same main idea.

Each of these two paragraphs starts on a new line and is indented.

Copy the paragraph below.
Remember to indent it.

Also in the 19th century, new equipment was invented for doctors to use to help them find out what was wrong with a patient. For example, they could listen to a patient's heart or chest with a stethoscope, and they could see broken bones with an X-ray machine.

Copy this passage about Louis Pasteur.
It is divided into two paragraphs.
Remember to start each paragraph on a new line and to indent it

Louis Pasteur was a French chemist who was fascinated by the tiny creatures he saw through his microscope. He looked at leaves, plants, blood, milk and cheese and found that these bacteria (germs) were always present in anything organic – that is, anything which comes from something living.

Pasteur experimented to find out why milk turns sour. He found germs in milk and he showed how the presence of germs turns fresh milk bad.

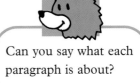

Can you say what each paragraph is about?

Now read this passage about Joseph Lister.
Divide it into two paragraphs, each with a different main idea.
Write the two paragraphs.

Joseph Lister was an Edinburgh surgeon. He read about Pasteur's work and wondered how germs might affect open wounds. If germs caused milk to go bad, they might have a similar effect on people. Lister experimented by putting strong carbolic acid on wounds. At first the acid was much too strong – it killed the germs but it made the wounds very slow to heal. He experimented with weaker mixtures of acid and water until he found one which killed the germs but left the patient unharmed.

Did you remember to indent both the paragraphs?

Copy these three paragraphs neatly.

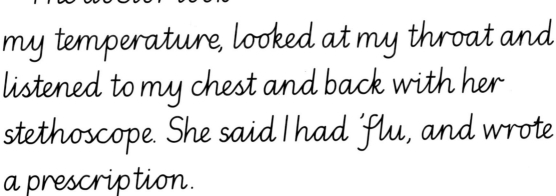

Last month I had a very bad cold which went on for a long time. My Dad made an appointment with our doctor.

The doctor took my temperature, looked at my throat and listened to my chest and back with her stethoscope. She said I had 'flu, and wrote a prescription.

I stayed indoors for a few days and took my medicine three times a day. I soon felt better.

The first paragraph was about why the child visited the doctor.
The second paragraph was about what happened there.
The third paragraph was about what happened afterwards.
Write three paragraphs about the last time you went to see your doctor.

How are you getting on? Look at the checklist. Keep practising!

Mr. Patel's car

We use an apostrophe to show that something belongs to someone.

children's pencils

dogs' tails

Write these sentences, putting in the apostrophes.

1 The boys shirt was torn.

2 The girls mountain bikes were new.

3 The nurses thermometer is broken.

4 Dad is in the mens darts team.

5 Mum went to the parents meeting.

6 The firefighters helmets were yellow.

Exclamation marks

When we write about strong feelings, we use an exclamation mark instead of a full stop.

"Wow!" said Jason. "Look at that sports car!"

Write these sentences, putting in the exclamation marks.

1 "Look" shouted the little boy when he saw the rainbow.

2 "Help Help" cried the sailors as the boat capsized.

3 "I hate salad and I am not going to eat it" cried Jodie.

4 "Look out" shouted the detective. "He is right behind you"

Sometimes we have to write very quickly:

taking telephone messages

making notes when reading

writing a note to a friend

brainstorming ideas

drafting stories

writing a shopping list

Copy the list above.
Can you think of anything else to add to the list?

Copy this shopping list quickly.

cornflakes	ice cream
butter	orange juice
apples	chocolate biscuits
bread	tomato sauce
fish fingers	baked beans

Your writing should still be easy to read.

Add five more items to your shopping list.

These directions were given to a lorry driver on the telephone.
Copy the directions neatly.

Turn left at the lights at the end of the High Street. Go along Queen Street until you come to a roundabout. Take the second exit and follow the road for about 800 metres. Then turn right into the street with a fish and chip shop on the corner. Number 43 is on the left between a postbox and a lamp-post.

As he listened to the directions the lorry driver made these quick notes.
Notice how he shortened some of the words.

At lights end High St tn left go along Qu St to rdabout. Take 2nd exit follow rd for 800m. Tn rt fish shop on corner. 43 on lt, post-box, lamp-post.

Copy the lorry driver's notes quickly.
Is your writing easy to read?

Try taking notes like these if you have to take a telephone message.

Copy these patterns as neatly as you can.

uuuuuuuu

wwwww
mmmmmm

KKKKKKKKKK
bbbbbbbbbb

Now copy each pattern three times as quickly as you can.
Can you still recognise the patterns?

A tongue-twister should be said several times very quickly.
Copy this one neatly.

The sixth sheikh's sixth sheep is sick.

Write the tongue-twister three times as quickly as you can.
Is the writing still readable?

How quickly can you write?
Find your writing speed.

1   Write this sentence as many times as you can in two minutes.
    Your writing must be readable.

Seven times nine makes sixty-three.

2   Count the letters you have written.
3   Divide the result by two.
    This gives you your writing speed in letters per minute.
4   Keep a note of your speed.

Now try again with this tongue-twister.
This time, write it as many times as you can in three minutes.
Divide the result by three.

She sells seashells on the seashore.

Record your writing speed like this and date it.

letters per minute

November 2nd

Try to improve on your speed.

A group of children were learning about the Tudors in their History lesson. They made this action plan for their topic report.

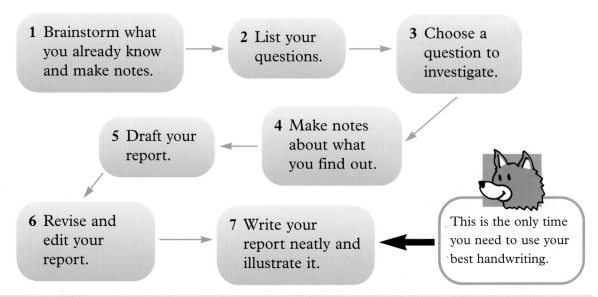

1 Brainstorm what you already know and make notes. → **2** List your questions. → **3** Choose a question to investigate.

5 Draft your report. ← **4** Make notes about what you find out.

6 Revise and edit your report. → **7** Write your report neatly and illustrate it. ← This is the only time you need to use your best handwriting.

Brainstorming

The children brainstormed what they already knew about the Tudors.

I know there were 6 Tudor monarchs, 3 kings and 3 queens.

Henry VIII had 6 wives.

Drake sailed round the world in the *Golden Hind*.

King Henry VII was the first Tudor monarch.

Sir Walter Raleigh was a favourite of Queen Elizabeth I.

Sir Francis Drake singed the King of Spain's beard.

Spain sent a great Armada to attack England.

You don't need to use your best writing, but make sure your notes are easy to read.

Make notes of what the children said.
Can you add any facts to the list?

Questions

The children made a list of questions, and decided to investigate this one:

How did Sir Francis Drake singe the King of Spain's beard?

Writing the report

The children read some history books and made notes before drafting, revising, editing and presenting their report.

Here is the final version.

Copy it in your best handwriting.

King Philip of Spain assembled a large fleet of ships in Cadiz harbour. His plan was to send this Armada to Holland to collect his soldiers and sail on to attack England. The daring Sir Francis Drake led his ships into Cadiz harbour and attacked the Spaniards. Many Spanish ships caught fire, and thirty galleons were sunk. Drake declared, "I have singed the King of Spain's beard!"

Did you remember to put in all the punctuation marks?

Letters should be set out clearly, and neatly written.

Uncle John has invited us to stay with him on his farm next month.

Oh, good! I'll write and tell him I'm looking forward to coming.

This is the letter Emma wrote.

Her address ➝ 14 King Street,

The date ↘ London SE3 3TY

March 5th 1997

The name of the person who will read the letter. ↘

Dear Uncle John,

   Mum and Dad have just told me that we are coming to stay with you soon. Can I help you milk the cows?

   I'm looking forward to seeing you! With love from

      Emma

Copy this letter in your best writing.

Imagine that you are Uncle John. Write a neat, friendly letter in reply to Emma.

Khayyam has been given the Jungle Adventure Game as a present. The instruction book is missing.

Oh, no! There's no instruction book! I'm going to write and ask for one.

Here is the letter Khayyam wrote.

27 Beech Road,
Glasgow G6 4GT
July 2nd 1997

Dear Mrs. Broad,

I was recently given the Jungle Adventure Game for my birthday. When I opened it I discovered that there was no instruction book inside. I would be grateful if you could send me one.

Yours sincerely,
Khayyam Daz

Notice that this letter is polite, but not as friendly as Emma's letter. Notice the different ending.

Copy this letter in your best writing.

Write a reply to Khayyam from Mrs. Broad.

Unit 13 *Speed writing in ink*

Whichever writing tool you are using, there are times when you will need to write quickly. Writing quickly in pen and ink needs plenty of practice.

Practise these patterns until you can make them evenly, smoothly and quickly.

wwwwww	wwwwww
oooooooo	oooooooo
ececececec	ececececec
wwwwwww	wwwwwww
amamamam	wewewewe

Daniel has made this list of things to take on holiday.
Copy the list. Write quickly, but make sure your writing is easy to read.

Baseball cap
Swimsuit
Books
Pens for writing postcards
Sunglasses
Cassette player
Flipflops
Snorkel

Can you think of anything else to add to the list?

Daniel sent this postcard to his friend James.
Copy the postcard, writing quickly but clearly.

I'm having a lovely time on the Isle of Wight. I've been swimming with my new snorkel and I've been to an adventure playground.
See you soon - Daniel

James Shore,
Flat 39,
Coniston House,
Glasgow
GE4 8SP

Draw some postcards in your book.
Imagine that you are on holiday, and write some postcards to
your friends and relations.

There are many times when we need to use print instead of joined writing – for example, when we are writing notices or posters, filling in forms or labelling diagrams.

This is the print alphabet.

Capital letters are the same as they are in joined writing.

a b c d e f g h i j k l m n o p q r s t u v w x y z

Copy this programme for a school concert.
Print as neatly as you can.

Victoria School Concert

July 1997

Reception	Some nursery rhymes
Year 1	The Owl and the Pussycat
Year 2	Robin Hood meets Friar Tuck
Year 3	Dick Whittington and his Cat
Year 4	Song and Dance
Year 5	The Naughty Boy
Year 6	Stanley meets Livingstone

On April 1st, the school cook printed this menu. Copy the menu.

SCHOOL DINNER MENU

April 1st

Solid soup
Grilled carrots
Roast cabbage
Molten beans
Drowned potatoes
Fried gravy
Scorched bread
Baked butter
Hot ice cream
Sodden biscuits
Stewed cheese
Toasted tea

Eat the lot
That's the rule
Knock it back
APRIL FOOL!

by Wes Magee

All the children in Years 5 and 6 voted to choose the events for Sports Day.

Here are the events they chose from:

Dressing-up race   Hop, step and jump
Egg-and-spoon race   Obstacle race
80 metres running race   Potato race
80 metres walking race   Sack race
High jump   Skipping race
Long jump   Relay race

Here are the events Ranjit voted for:

Ranjit Singh   Age: 10   Class: 7

1   80 metres running race

2   Relay race

3   Long jump

4   Obstacle race

5   Skipping race

6   Sack race

7   80 metres walking race

Copy Ranjit's list, remembering to print clearly.

Now make a list of your own.

Wayne wants to join a swimming club,
and he has filled in this application form.

Swimming Club Application Form

Surname	Robinson
Forenames	Wayne Jonathan
Date of birth	22nd May 1986
Address	17 Longbarrow Street Sumtown　　Postcode SU6 4ND
School	Victoria School
Address	Market Street Sumtown　　Postcode SU1 2TS
Hobbies	Reading, stamp collecting, model making
Sports	Football, cricket
Other interests	Acting, pop music, keeping pets

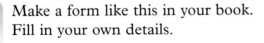

Make a form like this in your book.
Fill in your own details.

cold   chilly

Synonyms are words with the same or similar meanings. You can find synonyms for words in a dictionary or a thesaurus.

Copy these groups of synonyms.

unusual   strange odd peculiar

superb   excellent marvellous
           wonderful

weak   powerless helpless feeble

beauty   loveliness prettiness
           attractiveness

hot   boiling scalding scorching

cold   chilly wintry
           frosty

Choose one word from each group and use it in a sentence.

When you are writing, and especially when you are revising a draft, think carefully about your choice of words.

Definitions

$$\text{exports} \longrightarrow \text{goods sold to other countries}$$

A definition tells us the meaning of a word.

Read this passage.

Everywhere was <u>deserted</u>. There were no <u>pedestrians</u> on the pavements, no people in the parks. Everyone had <u>vanished</u>.

Match the underlined words with their definitions.
Write your answers neatly like the example above.

1 *people on foot*
2 *without people*
3 *gone out of sight*

Now write a definition for each of these words.

1 *shepherd*
2 *equator*
3 *thermometer*
4 *aquarium*

Use a dictionary to check if you are not sure.

A collective noun is used to describe a collection or a group of things.

a swarm of bees

Copy each phrase in your best handwriting.

a band of musicians
a crew of sailors
a herd of cattle
a gang of thieves
a bunch of grapes
a troop of monkeys
a swarm of bees
a pack of wolves
a plague of locusts

Now match these up and write the phrases.

a shoal of	eggs
a clutch of	corn
a gaggle of	trees
a forest of	fish
a fleet of	hay
a sheaf of	beads
a flock of	cards
a stack of	sheep
a pack of	ships
a string of	geese

Can you think of any more collective nouns?

41

A proverb is a wise saying which has two meanings.

The early bird catches the worm.

Copy these proverbs.

A rolling stone gathers no moss.

Out of the frying pan, into the fire.

A stitch in time saves nine.

Look before you leap.

One swallow does not make a summer.

Too many cooks spoil the broth.

Choose three of these proverbs.
Draw pictures to go with them.
Ask your friend to guess the proverbs.

Make hay while the sun shines.

Don't count your chickens before they're hatched.

He who laughs last laughs loudest.

A bird in the hand is worth two in the bush.

People who live in glass houses shouldn't throw stones.

When the cat's away the mice will play.

Every cloud has a silver lining.

All work and no play makes Jack a dull boy.

Copy the three proverbs under your pictures.

How are you getting on?
Look at the checklist.
Keep practising!

Writing with a pen needs plenty of practice.
Make sure that you are sitting comfortably
and holding the pen correctly.

Practise these patterns until you can make them smoothly and easily.

Copy this poem in your best handwriting.

The soft snow fell,

It made the whole world dazzling white.

The soft snow fell,

Transformed the whole world in a night,

Freezing the water in the well

Until the faint glow of sunlight,

When morning came and all was bright.

The soft snow fell.

by Edith Rogers-England

The capital letters for Nelson Handwriting are plain.
It is fun to use decorated capitals sometimes.

Here are some examples of decorated capitals.

These capitals were developed in Italy:

A B C D E F G H I J K
L M N O P Q R S T U V
W X Y Z

In the twelfth century the Gothic Hand was developed:

A B C D E F G H I J K L
M N O P Q R S T U V W X Y Z
0 1 2 3 4 5 6 7 8 9

Choose your favourite style of decorated capitals, and
copy these names in that style.

BUCKINGHAM PALACE
CANTERBURY CATHEDRAL
HOUSES OF PARLIAMENT
THE MANSION HOUSE
WINDSOR CASTLE
WESTMINSTER ABBEY

Have fun with
different computer
fonts. Many of
them are very
attractive.

45

For writing to look really attractive it must be well arranged and well spaced. Notice the generous margins (spaces) on each side of this poem.

Jamaica Market

Honey, pepper, leaf-green limes,
Pagan fruit whose names
are rhymes,
Mangoes, breadfruit,
ginger roots,
Granadillas, bamboo shoots,
Cho-cho, ackees, tangerines,
Lemons, purple Congo beans,
Sugar, okras, kola nuts,
Citrons, hairy coconuts,
Fish, tobacco, native hats,
Gold bananas, woven mats,

Plantains, wild thyme, pallid leeks,
Pigeons with their scarlet beaks,
Oranges and saffron yams,
Turtles, goatskins, cinnamon,
Allspice, conchshells, golden rum,
Black skins, babel and the sun
That burns all colours into one.

by Agnes Maxwell-Hall

Copy this poem in your best handwriting, including the decorated capitals.
Remember to think about spacing and to leave generous margins.

Here is a shape poem.
The child who wrote it thought carefully
about how to place the words on the page.
She also decided to use capital letters to
make her poem more powerful.

Copy the shape poem.

Now write a shape poem of your own.

How well have you done?
Look at the checklist.

Pollution

SMOKE SMOKE SMOKE SMOOO
SMOKE SMOKE SMOKE SMOOO

DUST
GRIT
ACID
RAIN
BLOW
WIND
KILL
MAIM
DRIP
LEAK
FALL
RAIN
ATOM
BOMB
BURN
FLAME
CREEPING CRAWLING
OOZING SEEPING
SMELLING SWELLING
WAILING WEEPING
TECHNOLOGICALLY SPEAKING
PROGRESS IS ITS NAME . . . .

You have come to the end of Pupil Book 3.
This is a good time to check your progress.

Copy this joke in your best handwriting.

What's the difference between a nail and a bad boxer?

One's knocked in and the other's knocked out.

Write these words and numerals in your best handwriting.

nought 0   five 5
one 1   six 6
two 2   seven 7
three 3   eight 8
four 4   nine 9

Write this sentence legibly as many times as you can in two minutes.

Four times three makes twelve.

Divide the total number of letters you wrote by two
to find your speed.
Is this faster than last time?